CELEBRATING HOLIDAYS

Christmas

by Rachel Grack

BELLWETHER MEDIA • MINNEAPOLIS, MN

Note to Librarians, Teachers, and Parents:

Blastoff! Readers are carefully developed by literacy experts and combine standards-based content with developmentally appropriate text.

Level 1 provides the most support through repetition of high-frequency words, light text, predictable sentence patterns, and strong visual support.

Level 2 offers early readers a bit more challenge through varied simple sentences, increased text load, and less repetition of high-frequency words.

Level 3 advances early-fluent readers toward fluency through increased text and concept load, less reliance on visuals, longer sentences, and more literary language.

Level 4 builds reading stamina by providing more text per page, increased use of punctuation, greater variation in sentence patterns, and increasingly challenging vocabulary.

Level 5 encourages children to move from "learning to read" to "reading to learn" by providing even more text, varied writing styles, and less familiar topics.

Whichever book is right for your reader, Blastoff! Readers are the perfect books to build confidence and encourage a love of reading that will last a lifetime!

This edition first published in 2017 by Bellwether Media, Inc.

No part of this publication may be reproduced in whole or in part without written permission of the publisher. For information regarding permission, write to Bellwether Media, Inc., Attention: Permissions Department, 5357 Penn Avenue South, Minneapolis, MN 55419.

Library of Congress Cataloging-in-Publication Data

Names: Koestler-Grack, Rachel A., 1973- author.
Title: Christmas / by Rachel Grack.
Description: Minneapolis, MN : Bellwether Media, Inc., 2017. | Series:
  Blastoff! Readers: Celebrating Holidays | Includes bibliographical
  references and index. | Audience: Ages: 5-8. | Audience: Grades: K to
  Grade 3.
Identifiers: LCCN 2016033346 (print) | LCCN 2016038328 (ebook) | ISBN
  9781626175921 (hardcover : alk. paper) | ISBN 9781681033228 (ebook)
Subjects: LCSH: Jesus Christ-Nativity-Juvenile literature. |
  Christmas-Juvenile literature.
Classification: LCC BV45 .K74 2017 (print) | LCC BV45 (ebook) | DDC
  263/.915-dc23
LC record available at https://lccn.loc.gov/2016033346

Editor: Christina Leaf   Designer: Lois Stanfield

Printed in the United States of America, North Mankato, MN.

Table of Contents

Christmas Is Here!   4

What Is Christmas?   6

Who Celebrates Christmas?   8

Christmas Beginnings   10

Time to Celebrate   14

Christmas Traditions!   16

Glossary   22

To Learn More   23

Index   24

Christmas Is Here!

Snow softly falls outside. **Stockings** hang by the fireplace.

The **evergreen** tree sparkles
with lights, and presents sit below.
Christmas is here!

What Is Christmas?

For **Christians**, Christmas is the celebration of the birth of Jesus Christ. Others share love with family and friends.

6

To celebrate, people attend church, give gifts, and sing **carols**.

Who Celebrates Christmas?

People all around the world celebrate Christmas. Families often gather for this holiday.

How Do You Say Merry Christmas?

Saying	Pronunciation
Spanish Feliz Navidad	fah-LEES nah-vee-DAHD
French Joyeux Noël	joy-OO no-EL
Italian Boun Natale	bone nah-TAHL-ay
Swedish God Jul	GUDE yool

Many different countries practice similar Christmas **traditions**.

Christmas Beginnings

The **Christian Bible** tells the story of Christmas. The story takes place 2,000 years ago.

Mary and Joseph traveled to Bethlehem. There, Mary gave birth to Jesus.

West Bank

Bethlehem

Bethlehem

N
W   E
S

Christians believe Jesus to be the **Messiah**. They began celebrating his birthday and called it Christmas.

Later, the holiday mixed with other winter **festivals** to form today's Christmas.

Time to Celebrate

Most people celebrate Christmas Eve on December 24. Christmas Day is December 25.

Many celebrate 12 days of Christmas. January 5 is called Twelfth Night.

Many Christians decorate with **nativity** sets. These show the Christmas story.

Figures include Mary, Joseph, and the baby Jesus.

Many people decorate
evergreen trees for Christmas.
These trees stay green all
year. They stand for life in
the dead of winter.

Make a Popcorn and Cranberry Garland

Many people use strings of popcorn and cranberries to decorate their trees.

What You Need:
- 12½ feet of waxed thread
- Needle (use with care)
- 2 cups air-popped popcorn
- 1½ cups fresh cranberries
- 2 small bowls

What You Do:
1. Thread the needle. Pull the thread through to double the thread, making a 6-foot length of string.
2. Tie the thread together in a large knot about three inches from the ends.
3. Put the popcorn and cranberries in separate bowls.
4. Push the needle through each piece of popcorn or cranberry in any pattern. Pull the pieces to the knot as you go.
5. Leave 3 inches of string when you finish.
6. Tie the end in a large knot. Makes a 6-foot garland.

2

4

Friends and family give presents at Christmas. Children may also receive gifts from Santa Claus. This gift-giver began as the Christian **saint**, Nicholas.

People spread joy and peace
at Christmas!

Glossary

carols—songs about Christmas

Christian Bible—the holy book of Christianity; the Christian Bible includes the Old Testament and the New Testament.

Christians—people who believe in the teachings of Jesus Christ and the Christian Bible

evergreen—a type of plant with needles that stay green all year

festivals—celebrations

Messiah—a king sent by God to save God's people

nativity—the birth of Jesus

saint—a person who is considered holy

stockings—sock-shaped pouches that hold small gifts at Christmas

traditions—customs, ideas, and beliefs handed down from one generation to the next

To Learn More

AT THE LIBRARY

Enderlein, Cheryl L. *Christmas in Mexico*. North Mankato, Minn.: Capstone Press, 2013.

Heiligman, Deborah. *Celebrate Christmas*. Washington, D.C.: National Geographic, 2007.

Ingalls, Ann. *Christmas Traditions Around the World*. Mankato, Minn.: Child's World, 2013.

ON THE WEB

Learning more about Christmas is as easy as 1, 2, 3.

1. Go to www.factsurfer.com.

2. Enter "Christmas" into the search box.

3. Click the "Surf" button and you will see a list of related web sites.

With factsurfer.com, finding more information is just a click away.

Index

Bethlehem, 11
carols, 7
Christian Bible, 10
Christians, 6, 12, 16
church, 7
countries, 9
dates, 14, 15
decorate, 16, 18, 19
evergreen tree, 5, 18, 19
family, 6, 8, 20
friends, 6, 20
garland, 19
Jesus Christ, 6, 11, 12, 17
Joseph, 11, 17
joy, 21

lights, 5
Mary, 11, 17
nativity sets, 16
peace, 21
presents, 5, 7, 20
pronunciation, 9
Santa Claus, 20
stockings, 4
traditions, 9
Twelfth Night, 15
winter festivals, 13

The images in this book are reproduced through the courtesy of: Smileus, front cover, pp. 16-17; FamVeld, p. 4; David Sucsy, pp. 4-5; DGLimages, pp. 6-7; Blend Images/ Alamy, p. 7; CroMary, p. 8; snvv, p. 9; Zatletic, pp. 10-11; beltsazar, p. 11; Marc Bruxelle, p. 12; kavalenkau, pp. 12-13; Christopher Futcher, p. 14; fotocraft, pp. 14-15; Pat_Hastings, p. 17; Alessandro Di Noia, p. 18; Lois Stanfield, p. 19 (all); skynesher, p. 20; RonTech2000, p. 21; Neirfy, p. 22.